Metamorphosis

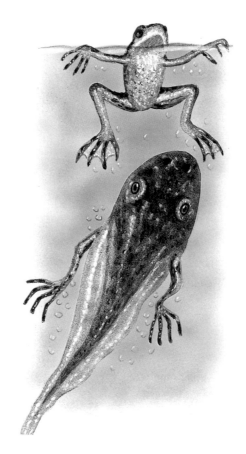

Andres Llamas Ruiz

Illustrations by Francisco Arredondo

Sterling Publishing Co., Inc.
New York

Illustrations by Francisco Arredondo
Text by Andres Llamas Ruiz

Library of Congress Cataloging-in-Publication Data

Llamas Ruiz, Andrés.
   [Metamorfosis. English]
   Metamorphosis / Andres Llamas Ruiz.
       p.   cm. — (Cycles of life)
   Includes index.
   Summary: Describes the process of metamorphosis in caterpil-
lars, tadpoles, and dragonfly larvae.
   ISBN 0-8069-9325-1
   1. Metamorphosis—Juvenile literature.   [1. Metamorphosis.]
I. Title. II. Series: Llamas Ruiz, Andrés.   Secuencias de la nat-
uraleza. English.
QL981.L5813   1996
591.3´34—dc20   96–9200
                                           CIP
                                           AC

1 3 5 7 9 10 8 6 4 2

Published by Sterling Publishing Company, Inc.
387 Park Avenue South, New York, N.Y. 10016
Originally published in Spain by Ediciones Estes
©1995 by Ediciones Estes, S.A.
English version and translation © 1996 by Sterling Publishing Company, Inc.
Distributed in Canada by Sterling Publishing
℅ Canadian Manda Group, One Atlantic Avenue, Suite 105
Toronto, Ontario, Canada M6K 3E7
Distributed in Great Britain and Europe by Cassell PLC
Wellington House, 125 Strand, London WC2R 0BB, England
Distributed in Australia by Capricorn Link (Australia) Pty Ltd.
P.O. Box 6651, Baulkham Hills, Business Centre, NSW 2153, Australia
Printed and Bound in Spain

Sterling ISBN 0-8069-9325-1

Table of Contents

Some animals undergo an incredible transformation known as metamorphosis.

As you can see in the drawings below and at the top of the next page, the differences between these animals' larvae and their adult forms are so remarkable that it is hard to believe they belong to the same species.

Thousands of animals live in and around a pond. Some undergo such extensive changes during their life that the body of the adult animal bears no resemblance at all to the body of the animal at birth. This process by which the animal transforms itself from one form to another is called metamorphosis.

Amphibians (frogs, toads, salamanders, etc.) are the only vertebrate animals that develop in this way. However, metamorphosis also commonly occurs in insects, such as butterflies and dragonflies.

Why do these animals change forms? By transforming themselves, they adapt their bodies to be better able to survive. For example, when there is a large amount of food around, caterpillars eat continually. They then turn into a chrysalis so as to give the plants they fed off time to recover.

TADPOLE

ADULT FROG

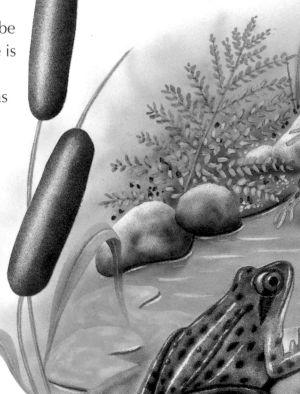

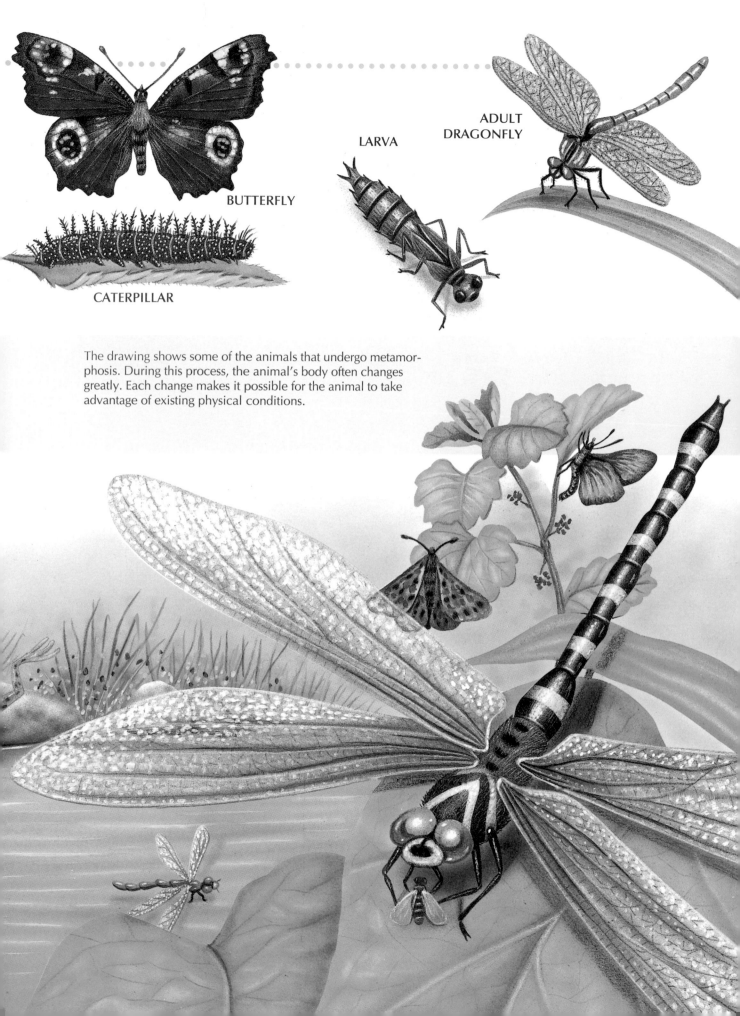

BUTTERFLY

CATERPILLAR

LARVA

ADULT
DRAGONFLY

The drawing shows some of the animals that undergo metamorphosis. During this process, the animal's body often changes greatly. Each change makes it possible for the animal to take advantage of existing physical conditions.

Everything starts when the parents meet and courtship begins.

When breeding season arrives (normally in the spring), some kinds of frogs gather in large groups of perhaps hundreds of animals with one thought in mind—courtship. The males arrive first and immediately begin their unrelenting croaking calls. You may have heard their noises! During courtship, males cling tightly to the backs of females (which are usually bigger). This embrace is known as amplexus and may last for days so that the male can fertilize the female's eggs. (The female may carry from between one and twenty thousand of them.) Thus, the frog's life cycle begins. In butterflies and dragonflies, courtship begins with spectacular aerial displays during which both members of the pair demonstrate their powers of flight.

To attract females, male frogs sing with all their might. Their expandable vocal sacs or pouches (one or two, depending on the species) help increase the power of their croaking. The songs are usually heard at night and each species has a different one.

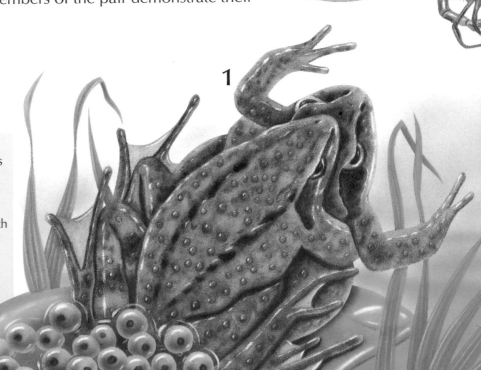

2

1

1. The male frog climbs onto the back of the female.
2. The male dragonfly grabs the female with claspers located at the tip of his abdomen.
3. Butterflies prefer to mate on a plant; they only fly off if they are dis-

During breeding season, some male frogs develop rough areas on their rear legs, which help them cling to the females.

Female moths send aromatic messages by means of pheromones. The males' antennae can detect these "love messages" at a distance of up to over 7 miles (12 kilometers)! Pheromones are emitted by the female while she is searching for a good place to lay her eggs.

3

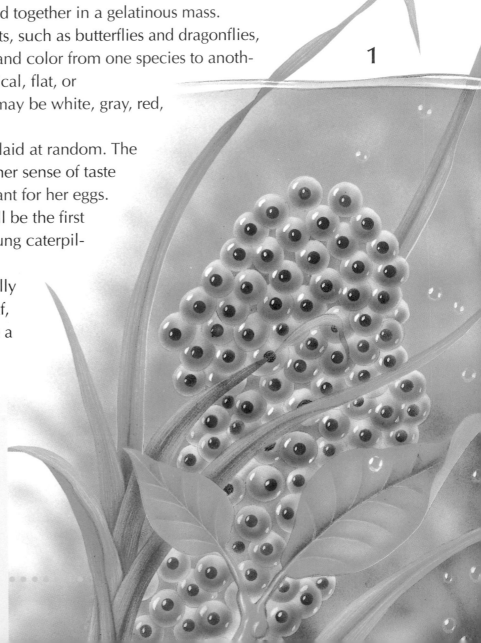

When courtship is over, the female lays a large number of eggs.

This male crystal frog, well camouflaged by the patterns on its back, is protecting a clutch of eggs from possible enemies.

Some species of frogs, for example, lay about sixty eggs. They measure only a fraction of an inch (1 millimeter) across and are grouped together in a gelatinous mass.

The eggs of insects, such as butterflies and dragonflies, vary greatly in shape and color from one species to another. They can be spherical, flat, or bottled-shaped; they may be white, gray, red, and so on.

The eggs are not laid at random. The female butterfly uses her sense of taste to choose the right plant for her eggs. After all, this plant will be the first to be eaten by the young caterpillars when they hatch.

Butterflies normally lay their eggs on a leaf, one by one, to ensure a high rate of survival among the young.

Many amphibian species lay their eggs grouped together in a protective mass of gelatin. These masses may take on various forms:
1. Frogs' eggs in groups.
2. Frogs' eggs in ribbons, wrapped around underwater plants.
3. Frogs' eggs in strings.

1

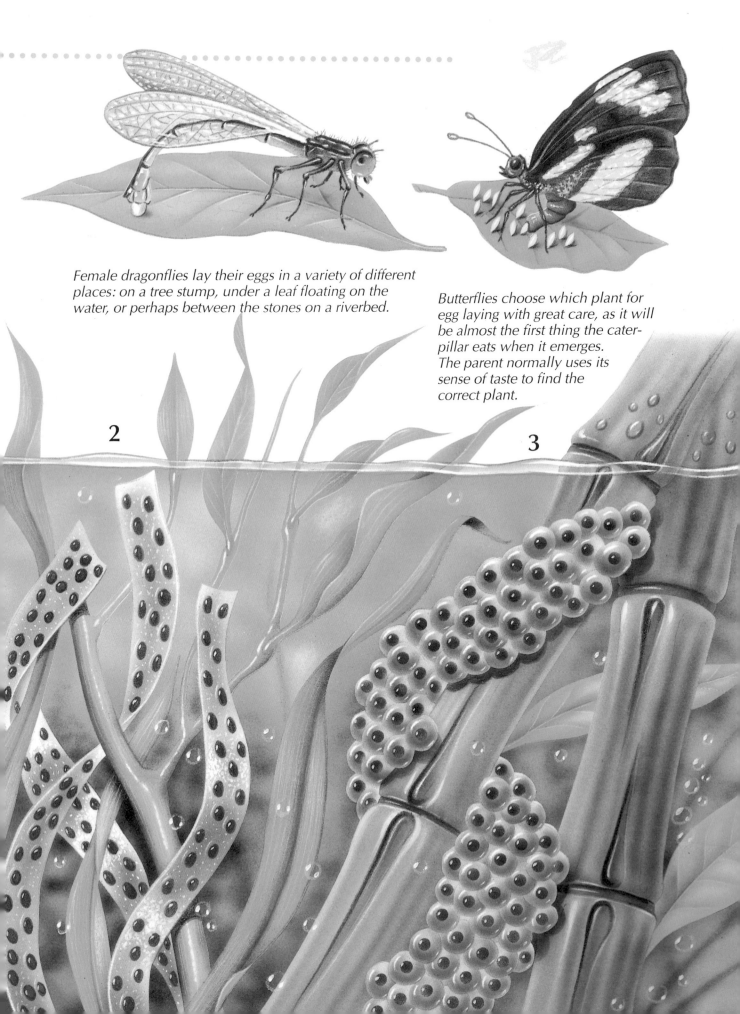

Female dragonflies lay their eggs in a variety of different places: on a tree stump, under a leaf floating on the water, or perhaps between the stones on a riverbed.

Butterflies choose which plant for egg laying with great care, as it will be almost the first thing the caterpillar eats when it emerges. The parent normally uses its sense of taste to find the correct plant.

2

3

As they leave the egg, these animals are embarking on a great adventure.

A

The egg, up to now a safe home, eventually becomes a barrier that the minute animal inside has to break through in order to "travel" into the outside world.

When the moment to hatch arrives, the tiny animal inside begins to move around and jolt the egg. Using a magnifying glass, you might be lucky enough to watch as a butterfly caterpillar hatches. If you do, you will see that the caterpillar has to use a great deal of energy to free itself.

First, it bites a circular hole with its jaws and then sticks its head out of the egg. The first impression of the head as it pokes out of the egg is that its jaws are enormous compared with the rest of its body. The head has to be large enough to allow the caterpillar to eat its way out of the egg.

Then, the caterpillar begins to wriggle and twist around to free the rest of its body. Once it's completely out, it eats the highly nutritive egg case.

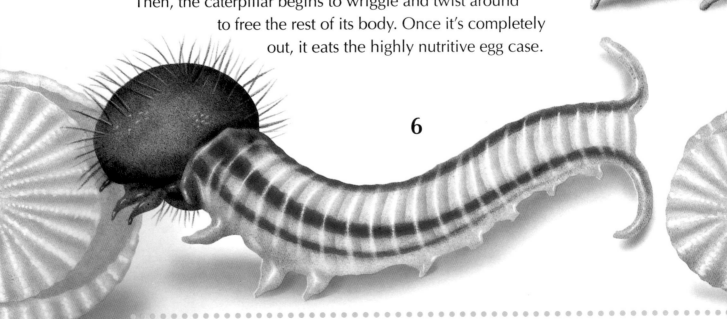

6

B

The female butterfly may lay different types of egg clutches: along a flower stem (A), in a ring around a twig (B), or on the underside of a leaf (C).

C

This male midwife toad is carrying the eggs on his back. For the next 3 weeks or so, he will look after them until they hatch.

1

2

How a caterpillar escapes from an egg:

1. A darkening or softening of the egg and movement from inside signals that hatching is approaching.

2. The caterpillar begins cutting a circular hole with its powerful jaws.

3. At last, it peeps its head out and get its first look at its new world!

4. Then it begins to twist and turn to free the rest of its body.

5. It continues to release its body completely.

6. Once fully out, the caterpillar instinctively searches for food and starts by eating its own egg case.

3

The female Surinam toad carries her eggs on her back. When they hatch, the young of this species are baby frogs instead of tadpoles. This is an example of development without metamorphosis.

5

4

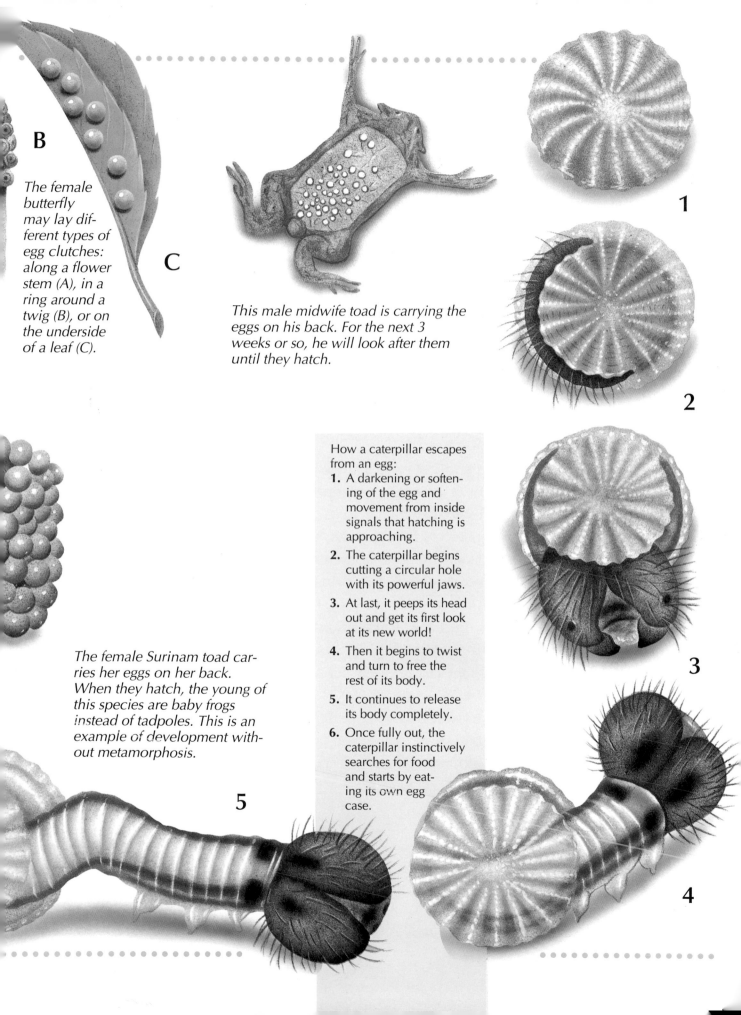

Some newly born animals do not resemble their parents at all.

Newly born creatures, whether they are tadpoles, caterpillars or dragonfly larvae, are always fascinating.

The eggs of some frogs are small and transparent spheres with a black dot in the center. As time passes, a lot of changes take place inside the egg. Eventually, a recognizable form begins to appear, jiggling around inside as if to say, "Let me out!"

About 10 days after fertilization, a strange being emerges from the interior of the egg—the tadpole, a creature that bears no resemblance at all to its parents.

At first, tadpoles move very little. Instead, they cling together to aquatic plants on the pond bottom. Suckers located between their mouths and bellies help them to hang on to the plants.

During the first few days, the tadpoles survive on their vitelline reserves. To breathe, they use external branchiae, which extract the oxygen they need from the water.

The tadpoles have to wait a week or perhaps 10 days before they can either swim, using their tails to propel themselves forward, or begin to feed on algae.

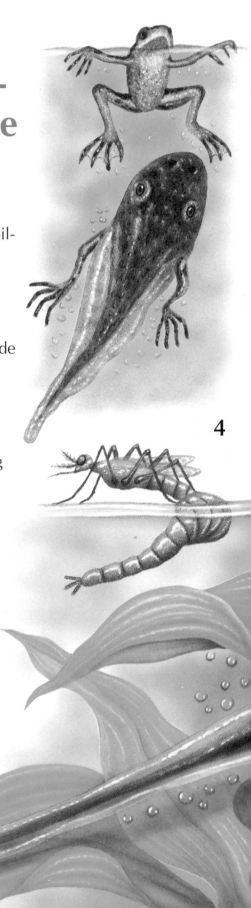

4

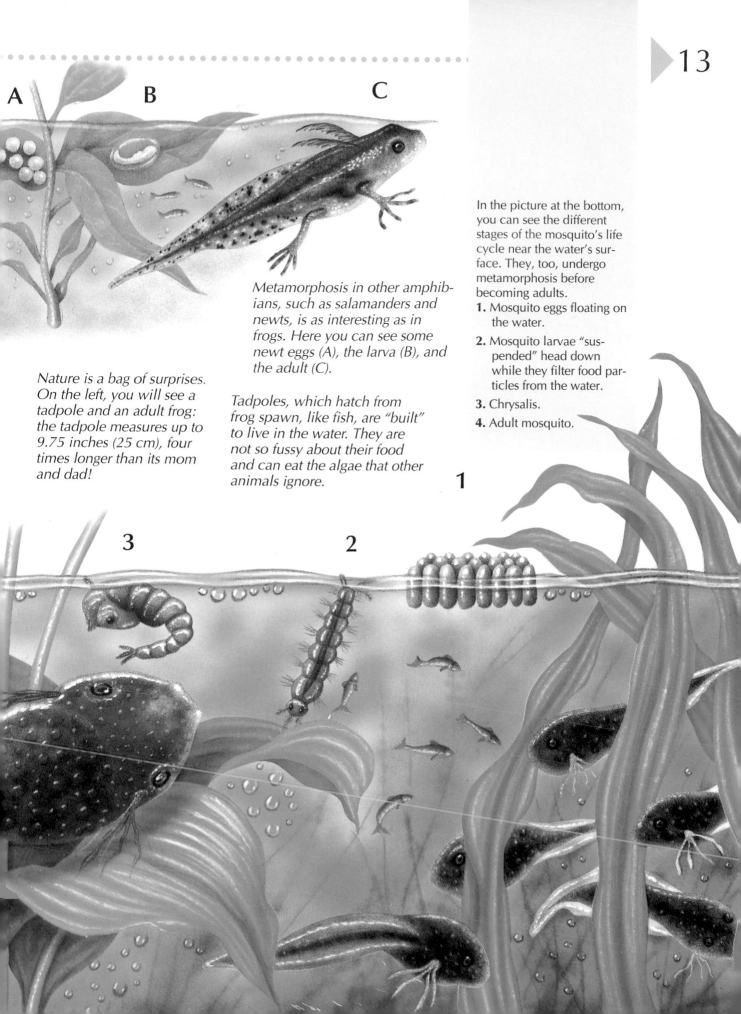

A   B   C

Metamorphosis in other amphibians, such as salamanders and newts, is as interesting as in frogs. Here you can see some newt eggs (A), the larva (B), and the adult (C).

Tadpoles, which hatch from frog spawn, like fish, are "built" to live in the water. They are not so fussy about their food and can eat the algae that other animals ignore.

Nature is a bag of surprises. On the left, you will see a tadpole and an adult frog: the tadpole measures up to 9.75 inches (25 cm), four times longer than its mom and dad!

In the picture at the bottom, you can see the different stages of the mosquito's life cycle near the water's surface. They, too, undergo metamorphosis before becoming adults.

1. Mosquito eggs floating on the water.

2. Mosquito larvae "suspended" head down while they filter food particles from the water.

3. Chrysalis.

4. Adult mosquito.

1

3   2

At first, caterpillars, larvae, and tadpoles are only worried about finding enough food.

As a result of their hearty appetites, caterpillars, for example, increase their weight ten thousand times from the moment they leave the egg until they lock themselves away in a chrysalis. They are not too fussy and will eat leaves, stems, roots, wood, and so on.

But don't think that life is easy for a caterpillar. Aside from eating, it also has to defend itself from its many enemies (birds, for example), which might be looking for a tasty snack. Like other insects, the caterpillar has to molt its skin to be able to grow; it will shed its skin four or five times before entering the chrysalis stage. When it is time to shed a skin layer, the caterpillar rests while the old skin falls off and the new, bigger one hardens.

The internal organization of a caterpillar is very simple: it has no lungs, breathing through holes in its sides. Its nervous system is very basic, although it receives sufficient information about what is happening in its immediate vicinity from its sensorial organs, which are small antennae and simple eyes called ocelli; they can detect variations in the amount of light. Nevertheless, caterpillars do have one thing that adult butterflies lack: a gland that produces the silk, which will be used at the appropriate moment to make the chrysalis.

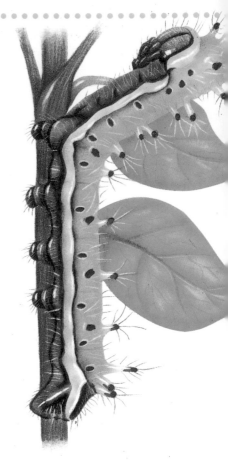

The caterpillar of the Australian emperor moth has hairs with irritating properties that contain toxic substances to protect it from predators.

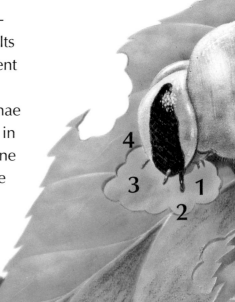

Not all larvae have to look after themselves. This male Trinidadian frog guards the eggs and then carries the newly hatched tadpoles on his back to the nearest running water.

This caterpillar is imitating a snake in order to scare off its enemies. It even has an organ that resembles the snake's forked tongue!

The caterpillar's body is perfectly adapted to be able to continue feeding right up to the moment it changes into a chrysalis.

1. Powerful jaws.
2. Silk-producing gland.
3. Short antennae.
4. Simple eyes, or ocelli.
5. Thorax.
6. Three pairs of legs on the thorax.
7. Breathing holes on the side of the body.
8. Abdomen.
9. Claspers.

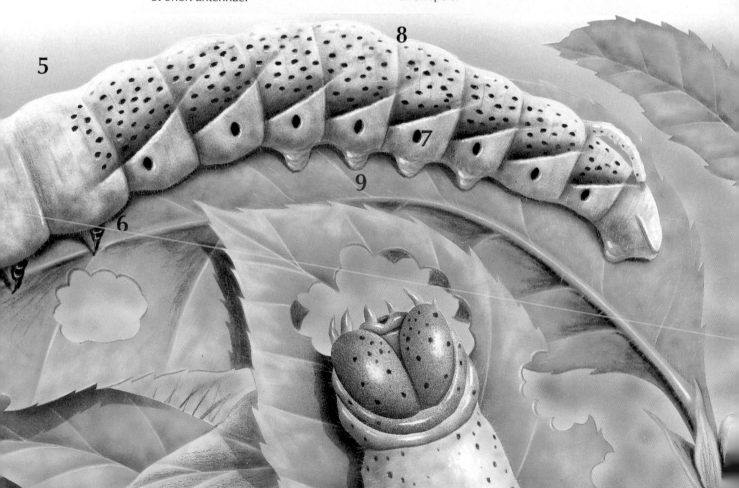

Dragonfly larvae are the most feared hunters.

Here you can see the body of a dragonfly larva in detail.

Dragonfly larvae are among the most active of all the invertebrate hunters that live in ponds and streams.

You have seen that caterpillars and tadpoles, just like other animals during their larval stages, basically spend their time eating (mainly vegetable matter) to build up the reserves they will need for the transformations ahead in later life. Nevertheless, of all larvae, one group stands out as the most ferocious hunters: dragonfly larvae. They look frightening with their well-developed lower lip, or labia, which is projected forward quickly to capture prey. The larvae also have large compound eyes, which they use to search out their prey. After birth, they pass through between nine and sixteen intermediate phases and will eventually reach up to 2.5 inches (6 cm) in length. The larvae of some species live for only 30 or 40 days, while others live up to 6 years "terrorizing" their underwater prey.

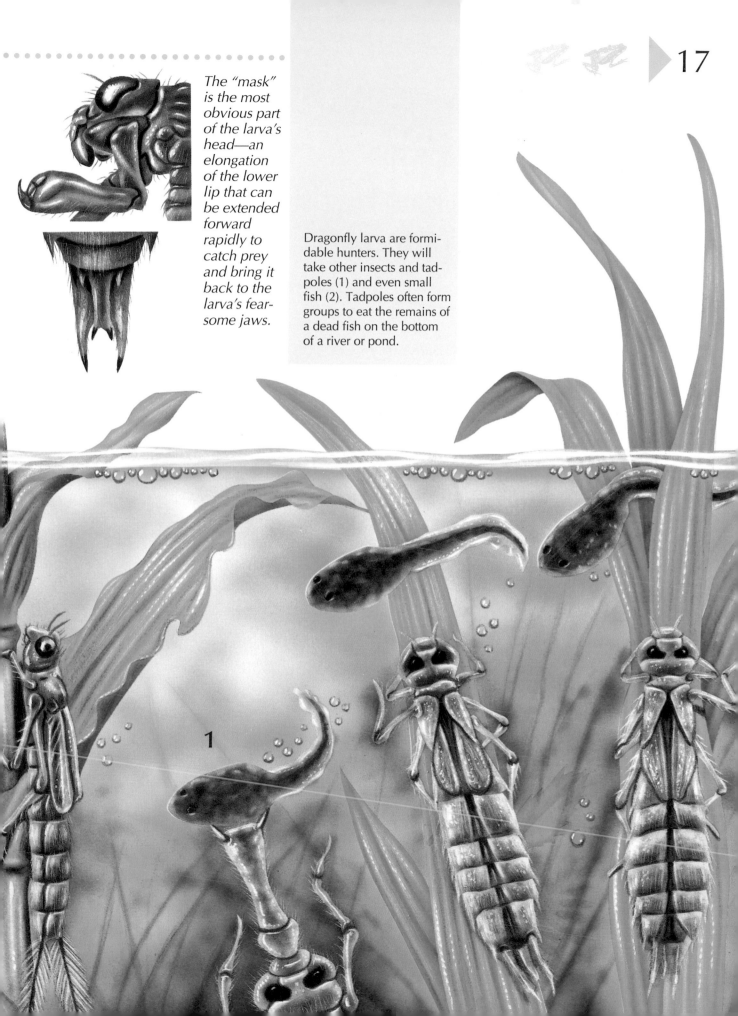

The "mask" is the most obvious part of the larva's head—an elongation of the lower lip that can be extended forward rapidly to catch prey and bring it back to the larva's fearsome jaws.

Dragonfly larva are formidable hunters. They will take other insects and tadpoles (1) and even small fish (2). Tadpoles often form groups to eat the remains of a dead fish on the bottom of a river or pond.

1

Meanwhile, changes begin: the tadpole's legs appear.

Tadpoles change gradually. After 6 or 9 weeks, their hind legs begin to grow. Small buds appear and gradually turn into functional legs. As the body gets longer, the head begins to separate and the tail becomes ever shorter.

When its back legs can help propel it through the water, the tadpole then begins to feed on small dead animals, such as insects and other tadpoles.

A few days later, the front legs begin to emerge. At 12 weeks, the tail is much shorter—essentially only a stump, which will soon disappear. This is when the animal leaves the water. But don't think that all tadpoles reach this point. Many fall prey to their enemies, such as carp, trout, tortoises, snakes, storks, herons, rodents, dragon-flies, and others. There are also many amphibians that eat tadpoles; parents sometimes will even eat their own offspring.

Once their muscles have grown sufficiently strong, tadpoles swim by using their tails to propel them forward.

In some species of salamander and newt, the larvae never change into adults! In fact, like this axolotl, they become sexually mature while still larvae. This strange process is called neoteny.

1. The tadpole at 4 weeks: The external branchiae are covered by skin; the intestine is long and convoluted. These tadpoles live in large groups and feed by scraping algae off the surface of rocks.

2. The tadpole at 2 months: The head is beginning to resemble the adult's, the rear legs help when swimming, the tail is long and flat, and the front legs are beginning to appear.

1

2

The caterpillar sheds its skin and turns into a chrysalis.

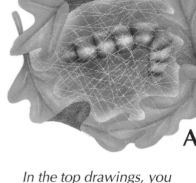

A

When the caterpillar has eaten enough, it begins to look for a safe place to transform itself into a chrysalis (also known as a pupa). There are different types of chrysalis: some hang from a branch, some are buried in the soil, some are wrapped in silk cocoons, and so on.

The caterpillar of the swallowtail butterfly, for example, takes hold of a plant with its hind claspers and makes a cushion-like support out of the silk produced by its silk glands. Next, it weaves a safety harness—or loop of silk— to attach itself to the branch so that it will not fall as the transformations begin under the skin. At this point, the caterpillar seems to shed another layer of skin as it twists and turns and the skin splits along its back. However, what appears under the old skin is the new skin of the chrysalis, which toughens up as it comes into contact with the air. Finally, the contortions of the caterpillar cause the old skin to fall off. The chrysalis remains totally still; inside, incredible transformations are taking place.

In the top drawings, you can see the sequences involved in the construction of the silk moth's cocoon:
A. At first, the silk web is very loose and open.
B. The cocoon thickens up.
C. The finished cocoon is made up of a single thread, 2640 feet (800 meters) long!

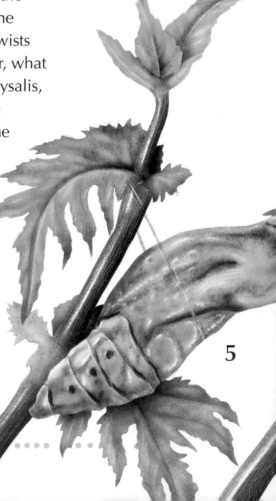

5

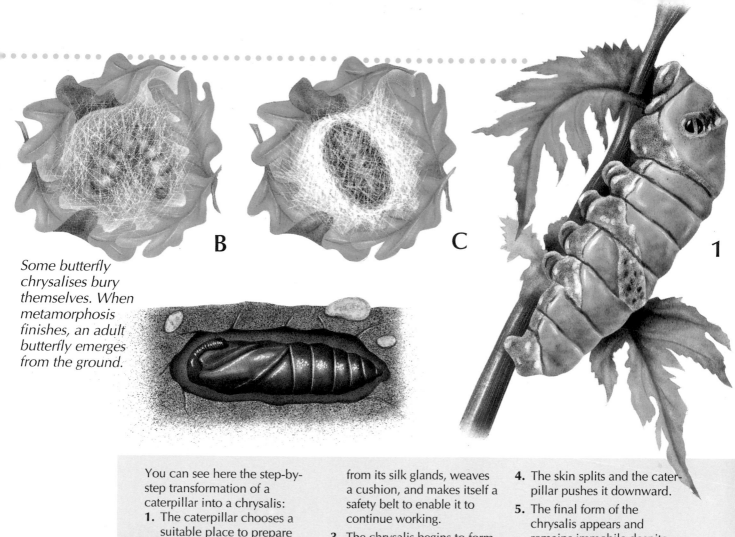

Some butterfly chrysalises bury themselves. When metamorphosis finishes, an adult butterfly emerges from the ground.

B

C

1

You can see here the step-by-step transformation of a caterpillar into a chrysalis:

1. The caterpillar chooses a suitable place to prepare the chrysalis.

2. The caterpillar produces silk from its silk glands, weaves a cushion, and makes itself a safety belt to enable it to continue working.

3. The chrysalis begins to form under the skin and the caterpillar wriggles violently.

4. The skin splits and the caterpillar pushes it downward.

5. The final form of the chrysalis appears and remains immobile despite the great changes going on inside.

4

3

2

Other insects do not form chrysalises; their larvae quickly grow to resemble their parents.

The most evolved insects, such as butterflies, undergo a "complete" metamorphosis during which their bodies change from a larva to an adult through a chrysalis stage. As we have already said, this process is relatively quick.

However, in some of the more primitive insects—such as grasshoppers, dragonflies, and damselflies—the transformations occur gradually, by means of a series of phases during which the larvae only slowly come to resemble their parents. We call this process "incomplete" metamorphosis, as there is no chrysalis phase.

Eventually, dragonfly larvae stop searching for food as the moment of the final transformation approaches. The larva's compound eyes have emerged, and the larva starts to look for a suitable place from which to leave the water. You must realize that the change the insect is about to experience is enormous: it is going to swap a completely aquatic lifestyle, which may have lasted for years, for a life with wings! Dragonfly larvae climb up the stems of aquatic plants or onto rocks or dry land, although most species need a vertical support to be able leave the water.

Three- to five-day-old sole:
• Fish fry live on the reserves provided by the vitelline membrane.
• 1.17-1.95 inches (3.5 mm) long

Did you know that there are more than five hundred species of flat fish but that none of them are born flat? Their fry look like ordinary fish and their transformation only begins on they are 2 weeks old.

Five-week-old sole:
• The cranium has developed quicker on the left-hand side.
• The skin has darkened in color.

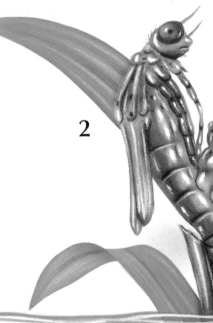

2

1

Eight– to ten-day-old sole:
- The spine is more developed.
- The fry can now open its mouth.

Two-week-old sole:
- It begins to feed by itself.
- The left eye begins to move to the upper part of the head.
- The cranium and the jaw begin to rotate.
- The transformation from a vertical fish to a flat fish is underway.
- 1.95 inches (5 mm) long.

Seventeen– to twenty-day-old sole:
- The left eye is in the center of the head and continues moving toward the right-hand side.
- It feeds on small prey, such as the larvae of other animals.
- 3.51 inches (9 mm) long.

As the last transformation approaches, the distinctive and, by now, completely formed features of the adult dragonfly can be seen:

1. The mature larva moves toward a plant stem and climbs up and out of the water.
2. Then it tightly grips the stem with its legs, holding on firmly during the whole emergence process.
3. Suddenly, the skin begins to split as blood pressure in the thorax increases and the final adult form slowly emerges.

3

A. Vertical but upside down.
B. Vertical but the right side up.
C. Covered by a cocoon.
D. Buried without a hard outer covering.

Meanwhile, funny things are happening in the interior of the chrysalis.

If one day when you're walking through the woods and you find a chrysalis, you'll probably think it's dead. In fact, its only connection to the outside world is through its respiratory openings The animal has to continue breathing while the adult insect is being formed inside the chrysalis.

The length of the chrysalis stage is very variable: the chrysalises of some species last a few days or a couple of weeks, while other species have chrysalises that may last up to 6 years!

Although the chrysalis phase is sometimes referred to as a "resting stage," the truth is that the insect's body cells are working as fast as possible to undo the old structures and to form new legs, new muscles, and all the other organs the adult insect will need.

Once the adult is fully formed within the chrysalis, the exact moment of emergence to the outside will take place when weather conditions are suitable. To avoid being born on a rainy day, for example, some chrysalii can forecast the weather by measuring atmospheric pressure and temperature.

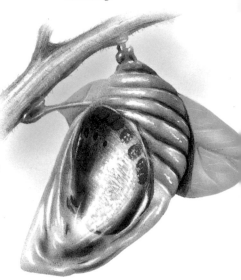

You can tell when an adult is about to emerge from a chrysalis because the color of the wings becomes visible through the outside of the chrysalis, which has become thin-

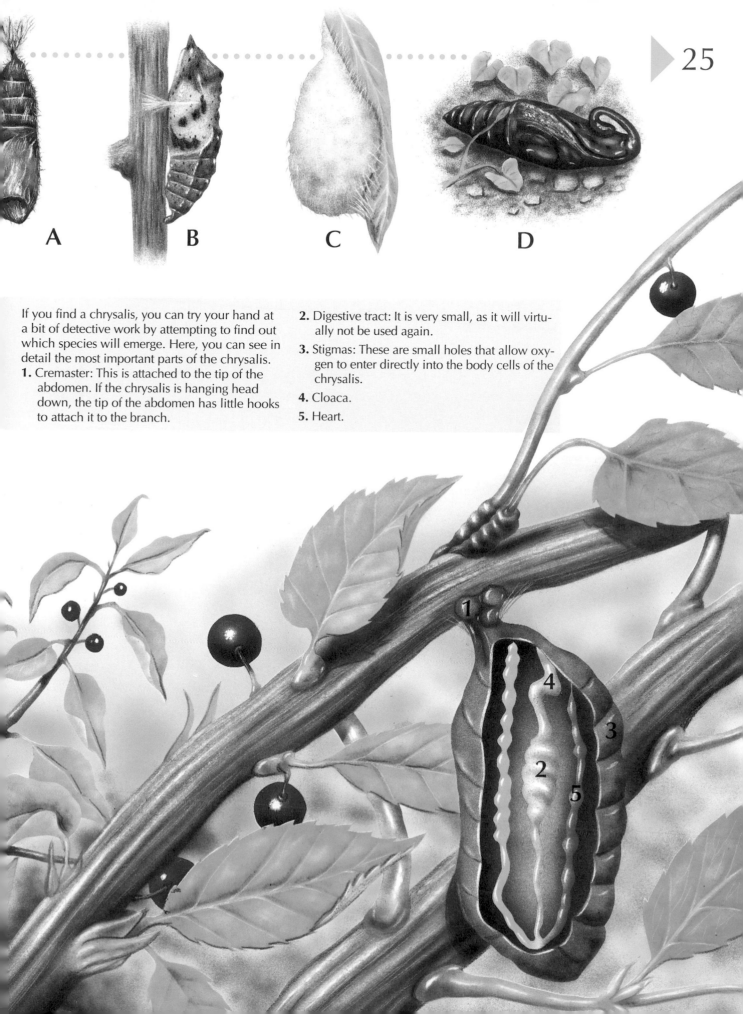

A   B   C   D

If you find a chrysalis, you can try your hand at a bit of detective work by attempting to find out which species will emerge. Here, you can see in detail the most important parts of the chrysalis.

1. Cremaster: This is attached to the tip of the abdomen. If the chrysalis is hanging head down, the tip of the abdomen has little hooks to attach it to the branch.

2. Digestive tract: It is very small, as it will virtually not be used again.

3. Stigmas: These are small holes that allow oxygen to enter directly into the body cells of the chrysalis.

4. Cloaca.

5. Heart.

The tadpoles are still growing and are looking more and more like their parents.

Eventually, the tadpole has developed so many adult characteristics that it is hard to tell if it is an adult or a larva.

Tadpoles take between 12 and 16 weeks—depending on water temperature and availability of food—to develop into adult frogs. If it is very cold or if there is little food, they may even hibernate as larvae and complete their transformation the following spring. They have small mouths with small, cylindrical teeth and eat plant as well as animal matter. They scrape or pull food off hard surfaces and can also feed on the fine layer of algae present on the surface of streams and ponds. In times of hardship, they will eat almost anything—a few even become cannibals if necessary.

As the tadpole grows, its mouth gets bigger and changes position, making it a better hunter.

Some smaller frogs leave the water without having re-absorbed all of the tadpole's tail. This frog from Costa Rica has just left the water and still has part of its tail. Doesn't it look strange?

Sometimes caterpillars carry around with them some very curious enemies. Parasite wasps inject their eggs into the caterpillar's body so that their larvae have a good supply of fresh food when they hatch. In the above drawing, you can see how around forty larvae are leaving the body of a caterpillar and turning into pupae.

Doesn't this 3-month-old tadpole look just like a frog with a tail? Well, in fact, most of the transformations have already taken place and it will soon be a tiny little frog.

1. The front legs are completely formed.

2. The tail is beginning to shrink.

3. The back legs are growing stronger and getting bigger. When they are fully formed, the animals' back legs will be strong enough to allow them to make the amazing leaps they need as hunters.

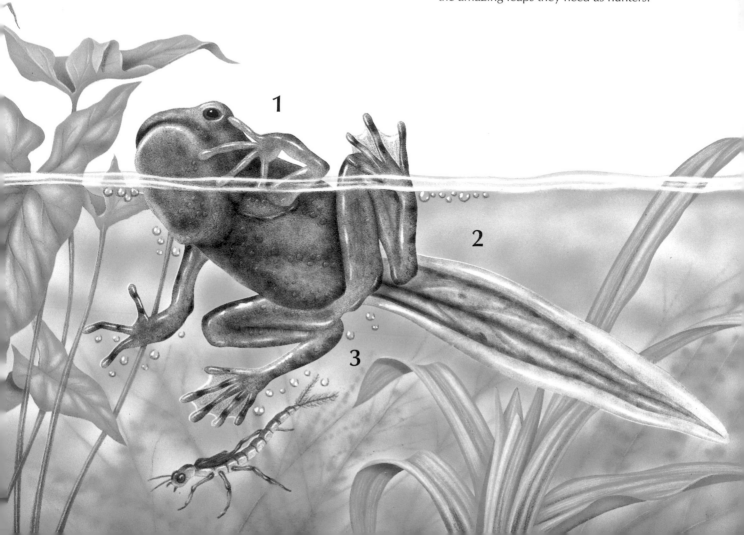

The tadpoles have become frogs, and now they make the biggest jump of all: out of the water!

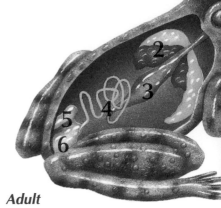

Adult
1. Large mouth without teeth.
2. Functional lungs, which allow it to breathe out of the water.
3. Stomach.
4. Short intestine (typical of carnivores).
5. Bladder.
6. Cloaca.

Here you can see the enormous internal changes that occur when a tadpole transforms into an adult frog.

Metamorphosis in amphibians is incredible. In a short period of time, the animal changes from what is to all intents and purposes a fish, to a "different" animal that is capable of living on dry land.

When the adult becomes a land creature and loses its fish-like characteristics, it also changes its diet. Adult frogs are carnivores: they lose their horny teeth, their mouths get bigger, and their intestines shorten to form a digestive tract similar to those of other predators.

Adults have very few teeth. But don't think this puts them at a disadvantage. Amphibians do not chew their prey; instead, they swallow their catches whole.

Eventually, the branchiae disappear and the tadpole begins to breathe with its lungs. Finally, the tail is re-absorbed into the body, and the tadpole becomes a frog, a little more than 1 centimeter long, capable of living out of the water and breathing atmospheric air.

During the last aquatic stages of its life, tadpoles spend more and more time at the surface of the water, breathing atmospheric air and preparing for the time when they will have to breathe out of the water.

Tadpole
A. Mouth with horny teeth for scraping hard surfaces.
B. Branchiae, essential for breathing.
C. Lungs, not used for breathing.
D. Large intestine to digest the food it eats.
E. Cloaca.

Once a tadpole has developed into an adult, it can begin to catch dragonflies. How the tables have turned. The dragonfly— once the hunter—is now the hunted!

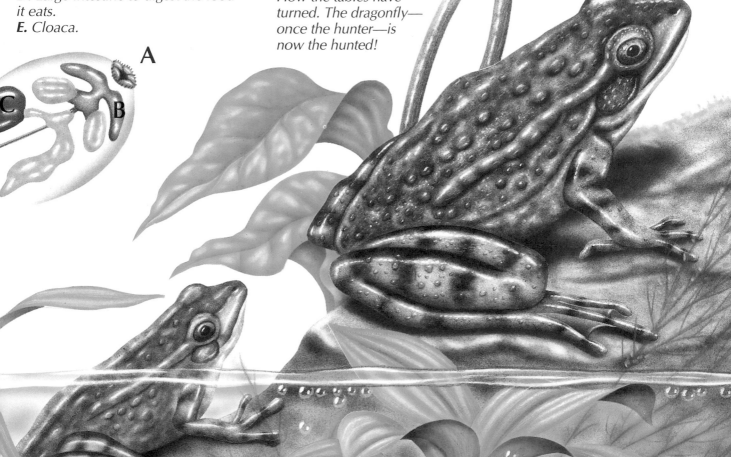

The development of the butterfly is over. Now it can fly!

The emergence of an adult insect from its pupa is fascinating. Some species of butterfly use a special liquid to soften the cocoon, while other species have a small saw for cutting an opening.

First, the butterfly breaks open the chrysalis and crawls out, unfolding its wings as it goes. Then, it begins to pump haemolymph through its wing veins, and the previously wrinkled wings start to stretch and flatten out, while at the same time its swollen abdomen deflates.

Next, the insect must wait for its wings to dry before it can make its maiden flight. It stretches its wings to make sure they reach their full size, opening and closing them a few times to complete the preparations. During a butterfly's short adult life (some live only for a few hours), it hardly ever eats; most survive on food reserves accumulated during the caterpillar stage. In fact, the butterfly's curious tongue is only used to suck a little nectar from flowers. The nectar contains only sugars (no vitamins or proteins), which provide the butterfly with energy to continue flying but not to grow.

The butterfly calculates perfectly how long to spend in the chrysalis and emerges at the best time of the year to coincide with the best weather and the plants in flower.

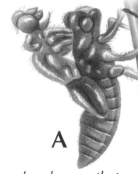

A

A. We have already seen that when the dragonfly larva is ready and environmental conditions are favorable, it too emerges from the water. Its life in the water is over.
B. As soon as it leaves its final skin, it extends its wings and pumps haemolymph through its wing veins and air through its tracheal tubes.
C. Finally, it chooses a sunny spot to dry and harden its wings. Now it can fly!

1

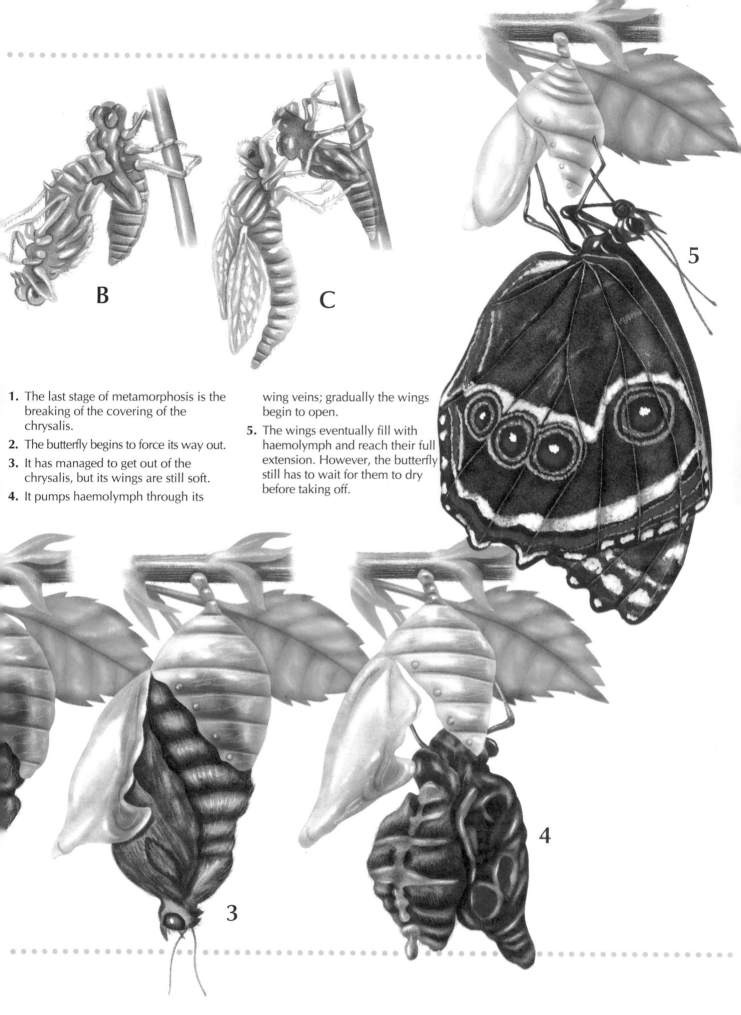

B

C

1. The last stage of metamorphosis is the breaking of the covering of the chrysalis.

2. The butterfly begins to force its way out.

3. It has managed to get out of the chrysalis, but its wings are still soft.

4. It pumps haemolymph through its wing veins; gradually the wings begin to open.

5. The wings eventually fill with haemolymph and reach their full extension. However, the butterfly still has to wait for them to dry before taking off.

5

3

4

Glossary

Amplexus: The mating position adopted by a pair of amphibians. The male climbs onto the female's back to fertilize the eggs as she lays them.

Branchiae: Respiratory organs in aquatic animals, such as fish, crustaceans, and tadpoles. In tadpoles, they are often outside the body.

Chrysalis: Pupal stage of a butterfly or moth, usually with a hard outer covering.

Claspers: Pseudopods that help to push food into the animal's mouth.

Compound eyes: Eyes made up of a large number of facets that are found in flies, dragonflies, etc.

Fertilization: Process in which the sexual cells produced by the male join those produced by the female to form a new individual.

Functional: How organs are described—for example, tadpoles' legs—when they begin to be useful.

Gelatinous: Resembling jelly.

Haemolymph: Colorless substance that circulates through the body of insects and other invertebrates. It is their equivalent of blood.

Hibernate: To spend the whole winter sleeping, without eating or moving, in order to use up as little energy as possible. Heartbeat and breathing slow down and the internal temperature of the body falls.

Larva/larvae: General term for a characteristic pre-adult form through which most invertebrates pass after leaving the egg.

Vocal pouches: Large sacs under the mouth of male amphibians. They help amplify amorous croaking.

Pheromones: Chemical substances that, when released into the air by an animal, make other individuals of the same species react in a particular manner. For example, the pheromones of female moths are a sexual call aimed at the males.

Predators: Animals that hunt and eat other animals.

Pupa/pupae: The stage in an insect's life when the larva is reorganized into the final adult form.

Silk glands: Glands that produce the silk used by butterflies and moths to form their cocoon.

Vertebrates: Animals, such as birds, reptiles, mammals, and amphibians, that have a backbone with vertebrae.

Vitelline: Coming from the egg yolk.

Wing veins: Veins that carry the haemolymph to the wings.

Index